Blue Ice in Motion

The Story of Alaska's Glaciers

by Sally D. Wiley

Published Jointly By:
The Alaska Natural History Association
and Judith Ann Rose

Alaska Natural History Association Publications
Coordinator: Frankie Barker
Designer and Managing Editor: Judith Ann Rose
Author: Sally D. Wiley
Illustrator: Sandy Frost
Photographers: Tom Bean
            John Cooke
            Alissa Crandall
            Brad W. Ebel
            Sandy Frost
            Rick McIntyre
            Bud Rice
            Greg Wiley
            Sally D. Wiley
Typesetter: Irish Setter
Printer: AdPrint

Published jointly by
The Alaska Natural History Association
Anchorage, Alaska
and
Judith Ann Rose
Portland, Oregon

ISBN 0-930931-06-8
Library of Congress Catalog Card Number 90-81062

Special thanks to Dr. John Edwards of the University of
Washington, Seattle.

Cover photo of Portage Lake and photo page 4 of Portage
Glacier by USDA Forest Service, Sandy Frost.

Contents

Dedicated to the naturalists
in Portage Valley,
whose enthusiam inspired this work.

Introduction

Glaciers. Cold, powerful, immense. Yielding only to the warmth of the sun's rays, these giant rivers of ice grind their way to the sea. Crushing everything in their path, glaciers scour the landscape, shaping mountain peaks and carving broad valleys.

Much of Alaska is locked in winter's frozen grip—where summer lasts only a few short weeks. High in the mountains, snow falls year after year, but it seldom melts. Glaciers dominate this rugged land, as ice once dominated much of the world. The evidence of their power and the spectacular beauty of their glistening ice give us a glimpse of the continual wonder of our world.

Rick McIntyre

The source, or beginning, of Muldrow Glacier in Denali National Park.

new words:
base
face
glacier
source / head
surface
terminus / tongue
terrain

About Glaciers

What is a **glacier**? A glacier is a "river of ice," a giant mass of ice and rocks that flows downhill.

Thousands of years ago, almost half of Alaska was covered with ice. Giant sheets of ice spread over the rivers and filled up the valleys. Ice also spread into many other areas of the world. Scientists call this the Ice Age, an alternating period of melting and freezing that lasted about a million years. About 10,000 years ago the world began to warm, and huge sheets of ice covering the land started to melt. As they melted, they left behind lakes, broad valleys, and a mixture of rocks and soil. Eventually the only ice left was high in the mountains. The glaciers you see today are remnants of the Ice Age.

There are so many glaciers in Alaska that no one has ever counted them all. Nearly 100,000 glaciers have been identified, yet most of them don't have names. Two things are needed for glaciers to form: lots of snow and a cold climate so the snow doesn't melt. The southern half of Alaska has the most glaciers. Just about anywhere in Alaska where you can drive or take a boat you can see these spectacular rivers of ice.

In order to understand glaciers, it helps to have a picture in your mind of what a glacier looks like. The beginning of a glacier, or the highest part, is called the **source** or **head**. The

glacier: a moving body of ice, a river of ice

7

The terminus of Columbia Glacier (Chugach National Forest) where it enters Prince William Sound.

source /head: beginning of a glacier
surface: the upper or outward part of a glacier
terminus /tongue: the end of a glacier, the most forward part

top, or the part that faces the sky, is the **surface**. The lowest part, or most forward end, is the **terminus** or **tongue**. The front end of the terminus forms a high wall which is called the **face**. The bottom of the glacier, where it scrapes along the ground, is the **base**.

How big is a glacier? Some glaciers can be very small—just a pocket of snow a few hundred feet across. Others cover hundreds of square miles.

8

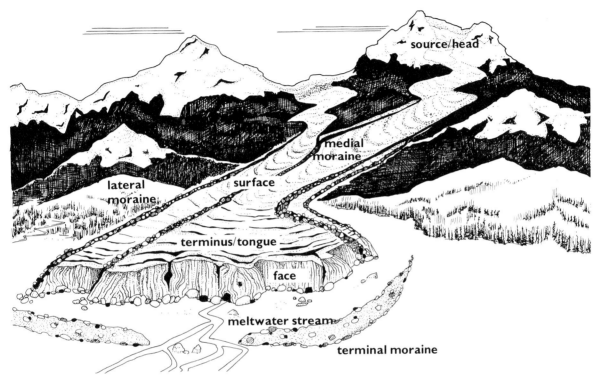

Glaciers vary in thickness depending on the **terrain**. A typical valley glacier might be 600 feet thick at its deepest point. This would be like piling 60 school buses on top of each other! Glaciers are deepest in the center and thin out towards the sides and the terminus. Scientists can measure ice thickness with a special radio that sends signals and receives echoes off the ice.

The parts of a glacier. (Moraines are discussed on pages 32-33.)

terrain: the shape of the land

9

Rick McIntyre

new words:
accumulation area
compacted
glacial
icefield
retreat / recede

The accumulation area, where snow builds up and feeds a large valley glacier.

How Glaciers Form

Glaciers form high in the mountains where the weather is so severe that snow never melts completely, even in the summer. On the mountain tops it can snow any time of year. Above 6,000 feet in elevation it stays so cold that no rain falls, only snow. Some Alaskan mountain peaks get more than 100 feet of snow each winter. Snow builds up in small bowl-shaped depressions in the terrain. It is here where the snow piles up winter after winter that the glacier begins.

Snow falls as tiny flakes, each with a different shape and pattern. When snow first falls, there is a lot of air space in the flakes. Then, as the snow settles, the edges of the snowflakes gradually get pressed together, or **compacted**—just like when you make a snowball. The snowflakes become smoother and more rounded. They lose their distinct shapes, and most of the air gets squeezed out. As new snow continues to fall, the old snow underneath gets more and more compacted. Eventually, the snowflakes become rounded crystals of ice. Water seeps between the remaining air spaces and refreezes, forming even larger crystals of ice. Some crystals can get as large as a soccer ball! Winter after winter, this ice grows until millions of interlocking crystals are formed, creating a solid mass of ice.

Think of the depression where the snow is

compacted: firmly packed together

Sally D. Wiley

*Most of the snow has melted from
the lower part of Raven Glacier
(Chugach State Park), leaving
the ice exposed.*

building as a giant bowl made of rock. The melting and freezing action chips away at the rock, making a larger place for the ice to sit. As the ice builds, it gets thicker and heavier, filling its bowl to the brim. Finally, the ice gets so thick that it overflows and slowly starts to slide downhill, becoming a glacier. Its own weight causes it to flow like a frozen river.

The upper part of the glacier receives the greatest amount of snowfall. It gains more new snow than it loses to melting and is called the **accumulation area**. The accumulation area acts like a storage tank for the glacier, and it is here the glacier begins. For glaciers that flow down a mountain valley, this storage area is called an **icefield**. As snow falls at the head of the glacier, it is compacted into ice and eventually flows downhill. New snow that falls on the lower part of the glacier usually melts during summer.

accumulation area: the upper part of a glacier where more snow falls than melts
icefield: a large collection of snow and ice that feeds a valley glacier

Individual snowflakes are slowly compacted to form rounded crystals of glacial ice.

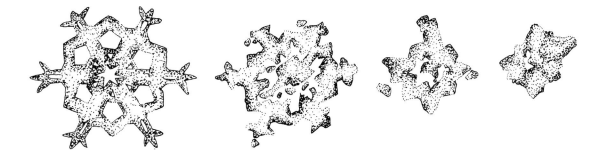

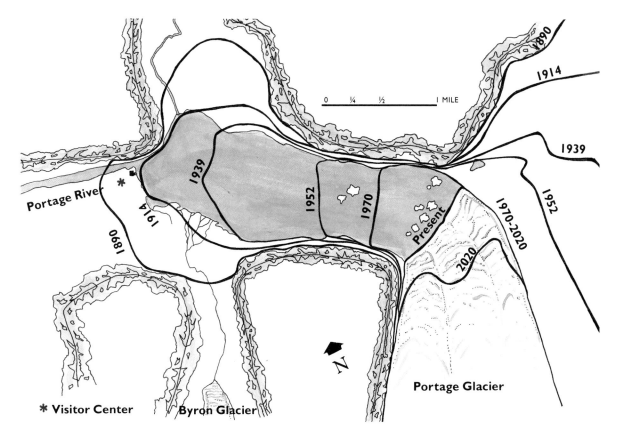

The following labels appear on the map:

1890
1914
1939
1952
1970
Present
1970-2020
2020

Portage River

* Visitor Center

Byron Glacier

Portage Glacier

N

0 ¼ ½ I MILE

The retreat of Portage Glacier
(Chugach National Forest).

Each winter snow falls on the glacier. Some of it melts, but most of the snow is compacted to form glacial ice. The addition of new snow "feeds" the glacier. Even though glaciers don't eat like we do, they must have a supply of snow to replace what melts each year. If a glacier is losing more ice than it gains in snowfall, the glacier is **retreating**, or **receding**. This means that the glacier is getting smaller because it is melting faster than it is growing. Portage Glacier near Anchorage is an example of a glacier that is retreating. This glacier moves forward about 400 feet a year, but 700 feet of it melts each year. This means the glacier is retreating about 300 feet per year. When people hear that the glacier is retreating, they might think of ice moving backwards. But remember, retreating just means it loses more ice than it gains.

Glaciers lose ice either by melting or by large pieces breaking off the face. Sunshine, warm winds, and rain all work to melt a glacier. When the amount of new snow equals the amount of melting snow, the size of the glacier stays about the same. If the snowfall is greater than the amount of melting, then the glacier grows, or thickens, and eventually advances.

retreat /recede: to become smaller

new words:
crevasse
deformation
glaciologist
meltwater
surge

Mendenhall Glacier (Tongass National Forest) near Juneau flows down its mountain valley.

Glacial Movement

Ice is a solid, but it still has the ability to flow. Glaciers continually creep forward as gravity pulls on the tremendous weight of the ice. You could stand at the edge of most glaciers from sunup to sundown and not be able to see them move. However, you might see a piece of ice come crashing down or hear the glacier creaking and groaning, clues that the glacier really is flowing downhill.

How does so much ice move? There are two different ways a glacier travels. The first way is by sliding over its "bed" (the solid rock on which the glacier is sitting). Because the ice is so heavy, it drags on the underlying rock. The pressure of so much weight trying to slide causes some of the ice to melt. This **meltwater** flows underneath the glacier, creating a slippery surface which helps the glacier slide. Meltwater is also formed from snow melting on the glacier's surface. It trickles down between the ice crystals or flows through cracks in the ice. Some of the meltwater refreezes inside the glacier. As the meltwater freezes, it expands, pushing against the bedrock to help move the glacier along.

Even though ice is very hard, it can change shape. This **deformation** is the second way that glaciers move. Ice crystals in the bottom part of the glacier collapse under so much weight. The

meltwater: water within a glacier created by melted ice or snow
deformation: to change shape because of pressure

17

Rick McIntyre

Crevasses split the surface of Peter's Glacier (Denali National Park and Preserve) during its 1986 surge.

crystals above them slide right over, much like a sliding deck of cards.

Glaciers are moving constantly, but they move at different speeds. While some glaciers move as much as a foot or more per day, others move only a few inches a year. The speed of a glacier depends on three things: the thickness of the ice, the steepness of the hill, and the climate. The thicker a glacier is, and the steeper the hill, the faster a glacier will travel. When a lot of snow falls, the glacier gets thicker and eventually moves faster. Whenever there is more meltwater for the glacier to slide on, it will move faster. The amount of meltwater in a glacier depends on how warm the weather is. Scientists are finding that glaciers start to speed up just before spring because all the meltwater that has built up during the winter starts to flow. By the end of summer, glaciers start slowing down because the meltwater has rushed out and left little on which the glacier can slide.

Different parts of a glacier move at different speeds. The center of the glacier moves the fastest. The sides and bottom move more slowly because they are dragging along the rocks. Because a glacier is a connected mass of ice, the terminus moves in response to what happens at the source of the glacier. If a lot of snow builds up at the source, eventually the terminus expands and thickens. This does not happen right away; it usually takes several years for the terminus to react to what is happening at the source. If the snow at the source of the glacier is melting, then the terminus eventually slows down and thins out.

glaciologist: a scientist who studies glaciers

Glaciologists have been measuring the movement of glaciers for at least 200 years. On Exit Glacier, near Seward, Alaska, markers have been placed in the ice. The movement of the markers shows the movement of the ice. The markers on

crevasse: an open crack in the surface of a glacier
surge: when a glacier moves at an unusually high speed

Exit Glacier move about 20 inches a day, or about 600 feet per year. Movement can also be measured by setting up a camera that snaps a picture once a day. The photos capture the daily changes in the glacier's movement.

Sometimes the glacier hits bumps in its path. Ice in the middle layer of the glacier can push up and over the obstacle. As the glacier forces its way over the bump, the top layer is stretched until it cracks. These giant cracks, called **crevasses**, can be as deep as 100 feet. Because they often lie hidden under snow on the glacier's surface, crevasses are a great danger to mountain climbers trying to cross the glacier.

The rate of a glacier's movement changes day by day and season by season. Most glaciers move at a steady rate, but occasionally a glacier will gallop forward at incredible speeds as great as 400 feet per day. The causes of glacial **surges** are not very well understood and almost impossible to predict. Some glaciologists believe that an unusually large amount of water at the bed of the glacier makes it slide faster—almost as if it were floating. These surging glaciers can travel a great distance in a short time. Suddenly, they stop and return to a normal rate of flow. Surging is one glacial mystery that glaciologists are working to solve.

TRY IT! There is an experiment you can do to understand pressure melting and refreezing. You will need:

a) a block of ice about 4" x 4" x 10" (Freeze a milk carton full of water; then, peel the carton away.)

b) a piece of strong wire about 3 feet long

c) two 5-pound weights

Set the ice block on a stand to support it. Drape the wire over the middle of the block so it hangs down over the edges. Hang a weight on each end of the wire.

Ice melts when it is under pressure. The pressure of the weighted wire should slowly melt the ice and cut its way through. (Be patient, it may take a few hours!) Eventually the wire will break through the ice, but the block won't split in two because the ice refreezes, just as it does in a real glacier.

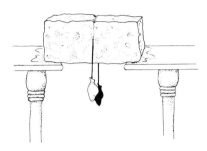

A weighted steel wire slowly melts through a block of ice. Will the ice break in two? Try it!

new words:
cirque
hanging glacier
piedmont glacier
tidewater glacier
valley glacier

When a valley glacier flows into the sea, it becomes a tidewater glacier, like these in College Fjord, Prince William Sound.

Types of Glaciers

Glaciers come in many shapes and sizes. All glaciers start high in the mountains, but they end in different places. While some glaciers end on land, others end in water. Some never leave their high mountain valleys, yet others spread out on vast open plains. Each of these different glaciers has a special name.

A glacier that starts from snow collected in a high basin or icefield and flows down a mountain valley is a **valley glacier**. Most of the glaciers in Alaska are valley glaciers. Some examples of Alaskan valley glaciers are Portage Glacier near Anchorage, Muldrow Glacier in Denali National Park, Exit Glacier near Seward, and Mendenhall Glacier in Juneau.

Sometimes a valley glacier keeps flowing right down out of the valley that contained it. Suddenly there are no rock walls to hold in the sides of the glacier. The glacier flows out and spreads out over flat ground. It then becomes a **piedmont glacier**. Piedmont glaciers are the biggest glaciers in Alaska. The Malaspina Glacier near Yakutat, Alaska, covers almost 850 square miles.

A glacier that sits high on a valley wall and doesn't reach down to the valley floor is a hanging glacier. Explorer Glacier (along the road to Portage Glacier) is a **hanging glacier**. These high glaciers are sometimes called **cirque** glaciers.

piedmont glacier: a glacier that spreads out over flat ground

cirque: hollow bowl-shaped area carved out of a mountainside by a glacier

A hanging glacier nestles in a high mountain cirque, which it has carved out of the rock.

Sally D. Wiley

tidewater glacier: a glacier that flows into the ocean

Glaciers that flow into the ocean are **tidewater glaciers**. The south central coast of Alaska has the most tidewater glaciers in North America. In Prince William Sound, over 20 tidewater glaciers flow into the ocean. The largest one is Columbia Glacier. Glacier Bay National Park in southeast Alaska contains at least 13 active tidewater glaciers. These glaciers are exciting ones to visit if you want to experience the thundering crash of ice falling from the glacier face into the ocean.

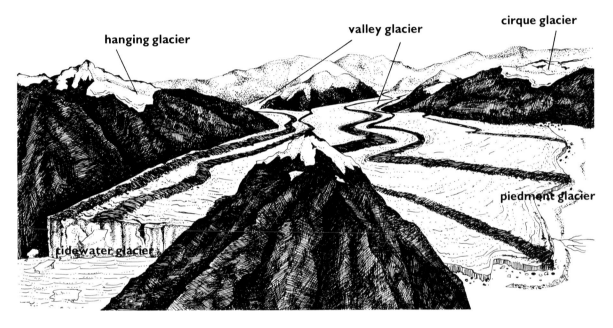

hanging glacier

valley glacier

cirque glacier

piedmont glacier

tidewater glacier

There are several different types of glaciers.

new words:
bergy seltzer
buoyant
calve
iceberg

A huge block of ice calves from Margerie Glacier, Glacier Bay National Park.

Icebergs

Imagine sitting in a boat on a warm summer day. You are on a sightseeing trip to get a close look at a tidewater glacier. Suddenly, without warning, a giant piece of ice breaks free from the face of the glacier. You hear a loud roar as you watch the huge chunk of ice disappear into the water with a tremendous splash! The ice pops back up to the surface and rocks back and forth. It is now an **iceberg**, a free-floating piece of ice that has broken from the face of the glacier.

Glaciers that flow into deep water lose ice much more rapidly than glaciers that flow over land. The terminus of these glaciers may extend several hundred feet below the water's surface. Deep water puts more stress on the glacier face, causing large chunks to **calve**, or break free. Ice can calve from any glacier, but icebergs are created only when the glacier flows into water.

Once icebergs have broken away from the glacier, wind and currents move them around easily, as if they were toy boats. Even though ice is **buoyant**, it doesn't float very well. Icebergs can weigh up to several million tons, with almost 90% of an iceberg's huge bulk hidden under the water. The hidden part of an iceberg can easily damage a large ship.

The appearance of an iceberg is constantly changing. Sometimes mysterious shapes appear,

iceberg: floating chunks of ice that have broken off the front of a glacier
calve: the process of ice breaking from the face of a glacier
buoyant: able to float

Mysterious blue icebergs drifting in the mist at Portage Lake.

looking like castles in the mist or pirate ships preparing for battle. Exposed to sun and water, they melt rapidly. In Alaska, the life of a large iceberg is about two months. As the iceberg melts, its balance changes. Giant icebergs can roll without warning, causing a large splash and sending shock waves in all directions.

How old is the ice that calves from a glacier? The age of the ice depends on how fast the glacier is moving, and how far it travels. People often think that the ice in Portage Lake is thousands of years old, but it is only about 50-100 years old. Portage Glacier is about six miles long, and the ice moves forward about 400 feet per year. It takes about 80 years for ice at the head of the glacier to reach the lake. While the glacier itself has been in Portage Valley for thousands of years, the ice you see today is less than 100 years old.

Some people think that ice from a glacier is colder than ice cubes from your refrigerator. Glacial ice won't make your drink any colder, but it might make it sizzle more! Glacial ice makes a loud "snap, crackle, pop" noise when the air that has been under high pressure escapes from tiny bubbles in the ice. This fizzing noise is called **bergy seltzer**.

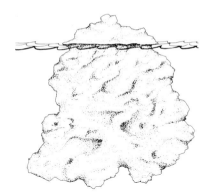

Only the tip of an iceberg shows above the water.

TRY IT! You can float your own iceberg. Place an ice cube in a glass and fill the glass with water. The ice cube floats, but most of it stays under the water, just like an iceberg. Fill the glass as full as you can without spilling over. What happens to the water level when the ice cube melts?

bergy seltzer: popping noises made by air escaping from bubbles in a piece of ice (also called "ice sizzle")

29

Glaciers have carved the landscape around Mt. McKinley (Denali National Park and Preserve).

new words:
erratics
lateral moraine
medial moraine
moraine
glacial silt /rock flour
terminal moraine

Patterns and Clues

Glaciers have tremendous power to change the landscape. As a glacier grinds its way down a valley, it acts like a giant bulldozer, moving rocks and soil and shaping the mountainsides. Even high, rocky peaks cannot escape the carving action of the ice. By looking at the mountains and exploring the surrounding areas, you can discover several patterns and clues left by the glaciers that tell of their passing.

As glaciers push forward, they scour the landscape, removing material from the valley walls and transporting it far downhill. Have you ever put your tongue on an ice cube tray or on a screen door in the winter and gotten it stuck? Just like your tongue, small rocks stick to the bottom of the glacier and are carried along. These rocks act like giant pieces of sandpaper, scraping and scratching the earth's surface as the glacier moves along. Years after the glacier has retreated, these scratches can still be seen in the bedrock as evidence of the power of moving ice.

glacial silt / rock flour: very finely crushed rock

As rocks grind against each other, they are crushed into a fine dust. The dust, as fine as flour, is actually called **glacial silt**, or **rock flour**. The silt is carried along by meltwater streams which carve channels or tunnels beneath the glacier. The meltwater carries the silt away from the glacier and deposits it downstream. You can

Debris left behind by a retreating glacier. This was probably a terminal or lateral moraine.

Sandy Frost

moraine: a jumbled pile of rocks and soil carried along by the glacier
terminal moraine: a moraine at the end or terminus of a glacier

see this rock flour if you look along the shore of a glacially carved lake.

Sometimes rocks get pushed along in front of a glacier. If the glacier retreats, it leaves behind a pile of rock which marks its farthest point of advance. This jumbled pile of rocks and debris is called a **moraine**. The word moraine means "broken stones." A moraine at the end of a glacier is a **terminal moraine**. A moraine can also form along the edge of a glacier as it scrapes the side of a valley. Rocks slide off the surrounding cliffs and get swept along by the moving ice. This is known as a **lateral moraine**. Sometimes two small valley glaciers come together and their lateral moraines join and end up in the middle. This new **medial moraine** looks like a dark stripe that moves far downhill with the glacier. If the glacier ends in water, and pieces of ice calve, they will often be coated with pieces of rock and dirt from the moraines.

The changes a glacier makes in the landscape remain long after the glacier is gone. When a glacier retreats, it leaves behind an obvious trail. Valleys carved by glaciers have a U-shape. Moraines become covered with soil and look like small rounded hills. Large boulders often are left stranded as the ice melts. These displaced boulders, called **erratics**, are a good clue that glaciers once covered an area.

Glaciers can sharpen mountain peaks, too. As the ice thaws and refreezes, rocks are cracked and gradually carried away, creating knife-edged ridges and bowl-shaped cirques. Patterns like these indicate a glacier has been at work.

lateral moraine: a moraine formed along a glacier's side

medial moraine: a moraine in the middle of a glacier, formed by the edges of two glaciers that flow together

erratics: large boulders left stranded by a glacier

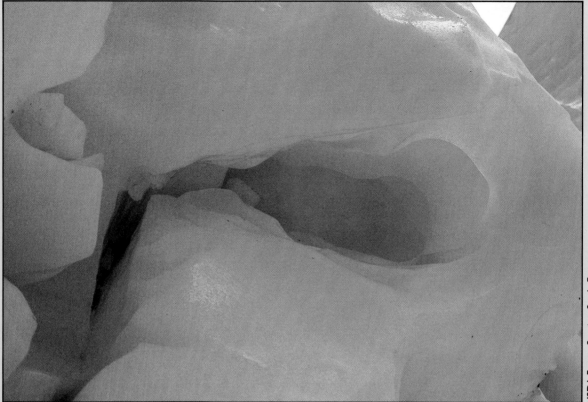

new words:
absorbed

The beautiful blue color of glacial ice. Here, meltwater flowing through the glacier has carved an ice cave.

Why is the Ice Blue?

If you have ever visited a glacier, you have probably noticed that glacial ice is often a deep blue color. This is because of the way light passes through the ice. Light that you see from the sun is visible light, or white light. This light is really made up of all the colors of the rainbow. Each color has a different amount of energy. Remember that glacier ice is made of solid crystals that have very little space between them. White light striking the ice crystals doesn't escape but is scattered into a rainbow of colors. Colors like red and yellow have a low energy level, and thus are **absorbed** by the thick ice. Because of the way ice is formed, it absorbs red light more than blue. Blue light has enough energy to escape the ice so that you can see it. As a result, when sunlight strikes the ice with all the colors, blue is the only one that you see.

You can get a close-up view of blue ice at many Alaskan glaciers, including Portage Glacier, Exit Glacier, Mendenhall Glacier, and the tidewater glaciers of Prince William Sound and Glacier Bay National Park.

Not all glacial ice looks blue, however. Ice with lots of air bubbles reflects white light, so it looks white. If white light can pass all the way through a piece of ice, the ice will appear white. On the glacier, snow, rocks, and dirt get mixed

absorbed: to take in, like a sponge would soak up water

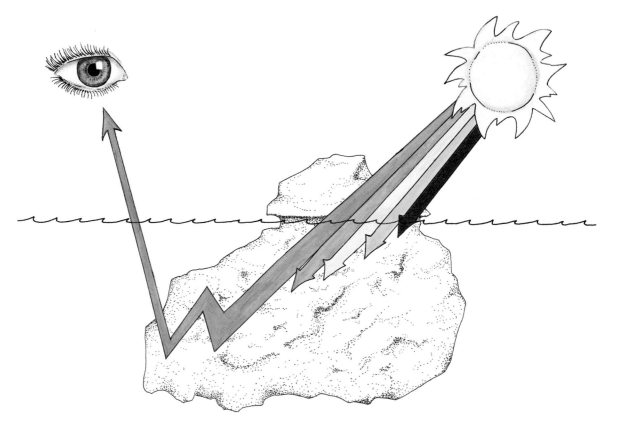

White light is made up of many colors. Blue light escapes from the ice crystals and makes the ice look blue.

in with the ice which can appear any shade from bright white to dirty gray.

Many glacial lakes have a deep blue color even on a cloudy day. The glacial silt carried off the glacier floats in the water and reflects blue light. When there is a lot of silt in the water, the water looks milky-gray.

TRY IT! You can make your own rainbow of colors to help you understand the light spectrum. You will need: a sunny day, a blank piece of paper, and a prism (your school may have one.) Find a place where the sun shines through the window. Place the piece of paper on a table so that the sun's rays are shining on it. Hold the prism in the light and turn it until you get a rainbow on the paper. Trace the colors with colored pencils or crayons. Crystals of glacial ice act just like giant prisms to break up the white light. The red end of the spectrum is absorbed by the ice, and blue is reflected. What happens to the purple color?

Bud Rice

new words:
debris
iceworm

Seals rest on a floating iceberg in Prince William Sound. Baby seals are born on the ice where they are safe from danger.

Life on a Glacier

Is there life on a glacier?

Twisted and folded by stress, the surface of a glacier is a jumble of rocks and dirty snow. Up close, it looks like a barren wasteland, cold and uninviting. What could possibly live in such a harsh place where the snow blows and the wind howls? Amazingly enough, it is the wind that brings life to the glacier. As wind moves over the land, it gathers up bits of dust and **debris**. When the wind sweeps over the glacier, it drops part of this load. Mixed in with the dust are tiny insects, bacteria, minerals, and grains of pollen from flowers. These are spread over the snow and ice, becoming a feast for tiny creatures such as the snow flea, an insect that crawls around on the glacier in search of pollen.

Many tales are told of tiny worms that live hidden in the cold glacial ice. **Iceworms** do indeed exist, and they depend mainly on the wind to bring their dinner of pollen and other plant materials. Iceworms are a relative of the earthworm, but are less than an inch long. They wriggle between ice crystals near the glacier's surface, sometimes as deep as six feet.

Iceworms burrow into the glacier's ice during the heat of the day and inch to the surface around dusk to feed. They lay their eggs right in the ice, and it is there that the young iceworms hatch.

debris: loose pieces of rock, soil, and other materials
iceworm: a tiny worm that lives in glacier ice

Tiny iceworms gather on a glacier's surface, looking like pieces of black thread.

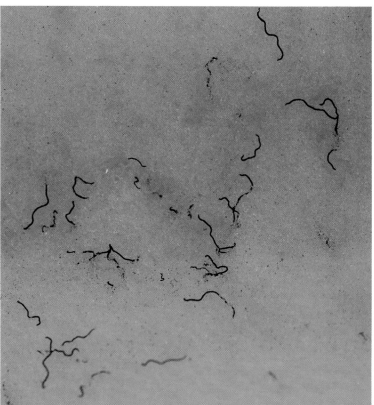

John Cooke

A magnified view of iceworms taken in a laboratory. Here they look much like their earthworm cousins.

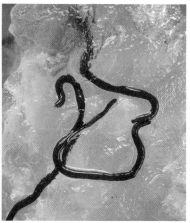

John Cooke

40

Sometimes it is possible to find as many as 100 iceworms in one spot on top of the glacier, while other areas won't have any. If you are lucky enough to visit a glacier where you can get close to the ice, try turning over some rocks or looking in small pools of water on the glacier's surface near dusk. Few people are fortunate enough to see these tiny creatures, and some don't even believe that they are real!

Iceworms can only survive under certain conditions. Temperatures around freezing (32°F.) are perfect. If iceworms get caught in the sun's heat where it is warmer than 40°F., they will die. If the ice around them freezes solid and becomes colder than 22°F., their bodies freeze. Iceworms are found only in glaciers near the ocean, or where the climate is warm enough for meltwater to be in the ice at all times.

Iceworms also feed on a special algae plant that grows on the snow surface. Most algae is green, but snow algae is red. The red color provides a screen against the sun's bright rays. Like other plants, red algae produces its own food. Sometimes it grows and spreads so thickly that it makes the snow look blush-red.

Along with the dust blown onto the glacier come spiders, beetles, flies, and other insects. Some of these find food, but others become food for larger animals. Birds flying over the glacier

*A bald eagle watches for a meal
from its perch on a giant iceberg.*

feed on iceworms and insects, plucking them from the ice.

Other animals use glaciers as a temporary home. On tidewater glaciers like Columbia Glacier, where the ice tumbles into the ocean, seals will crawl onto the icebergs to have their babies. The young seal pups and their mothers can rest on the icebergs, safe from predators. Eagles often perch on the large icebergs, watching for fish or other prey.

On some glaciers, the ice at the terminus becomes buried by rock debris that has fallen on the surface. After enough dirt builds up, it insulates the ice and slows down the melting. Here, plants can grow and animals can find food. The tip of Muldrow Glacier in Denali National Park is an example of a "buried" glacier.

The world of a glacier is a cold and desolate one where only the hearty survive. For those creatures that have learned to live in the harsh conditions, however, the frigid ice provides both a home and a resting place.

Sandy Frost

**new words:
global warming
precipitation**

High in the mountains precipitation falls mainly as snow, and seldom melts.

Glaciers and the Future

People have been fascinated by glaciers for a long time. The spectacular beauty of Alaska's glaciers delights thousands of visitors every year. Beautiful as they are, glaciers are also an important natural feature. Glaciers hold 77% of the fresh water in the world. Communities at the foot of large mountains use glaciers as a source of water. In some areas, power companies use glacial rivers to make electricity. Some dry countries are looking at ways to transport glacial ice for a source of fresh water. Glacial ice has a reputation for being crystal clear and extra cold.

Glaciers are a natural data bank. In between their layers of compacted snow, they hold records of volcanic eruptions, chemicals in the air, and changes in the atmosphere. They reflect changes in weather and climate over long periods of time. By studying glaciers, scientists can learn many things about our changing environment and can help us predict future changes.

Great concern is voiced in the world today about **global warming**. A slight increase in world temperature could have serious effects on our weather. Scientists have predicted that world temperatures will warm about five degrees in the next century or two. For Alaskan glaciers, this means ideal conditions for growth. As temperatures increase, so does **precipitation**, which in

global warming: an increase in world temperatures related to heat trapped by increased carbon dioxide in our atmosphere, especially in the last 150 years

precipitation: amount of water that has fallen from the sky in forms such as rain, snow, and hail.

The future of glaciers is uncertain, but we can value their beauty and the information they can provide.

© 1989 Alissa Crandall

the high mountains falls in the form of snow. Several glaciers in the Chugach Mountains area have grown thicker in the past few years. The ends of these glaciers are still receding, but the tops are thickening, and eventually they will advance. Many scientists think that the past Ice Age is not over. They believe that we are merely in one of the warmer periods, and the return of the ice is inevitable.

On the other hand, if world temperatures increase as much as ten degrees, snowfall in the mountains would turn to rain, and the glaciers would begin to melt. If all the glaciers in the world started melting, the level of the oceans would rise, flooding many coastal cities.

We have the power to control the activities of humans so that the balance of nature is not destroyed. However, we do not have the power to prevent the flow of glaciers if they begin to reclaim the land. We will not see another Ice Age during our lifetime, but the earth is continually changing. We have only begun to understand what glaciers have to tell us. Scientists will continue to study glaciers, hoping to learn more about our changing environment. We do not know what will happen to glaciers in the future, but it is the mystery of the towering walls of blue ice that continues to fascinate us.

* BARROW

Arctic Ocean

* PRUDHOE BAY

Brooks Range

* NOME

Arctic Circle

* FAIRBANKS

* BETHEL

• Muldrow Glacier

• Matanuska Glacier

ANCHORAGE

Columbia Glacier

Portage Glacier • * VALDEZ

Exit Glacier • * CORDOVA

SEWARD • Childs Glacier

Bristol Bay

Prince William Sound

Malaspina Glacier • Hubbard Glacier

* KODIAK

YAKUTAT *

Glacier Bay

• Mendenhall Glacier

* JUNEAU

Gulf of Alaska

PETERSBURG

SITKA * *

* WRANGELL

* KETCHIKAN

ALASKA

To learn more about glaciers, read:

Alaska's Glaciers. Alaska Geographic. Vol. 9 No. 1. 1982.
Glaciers and Icecaps. by Martyn Bramwell. Earth Science Library.
  Franklin Watts Inc. New York. 1986.
Glaciers: A New True Book. by D.V. Georges. Children's Press,
  Chicago. 1986.
Icebergs and Glaciers. by Seymour Simon. William Morrow and Co.
  Inc. New York. 1987.
Mendenhall Glacier: A River of Ice. by Scott Foster. Alaska Natural
  History Association, Anchorage. 1988.
The Power of Ice. by Ruth Radlauer and Lisa Sue Gitkin. Children's
  Press, Chicago. 1985.

or write:

Alaska Public Lands Information Center
605 W. 4th Ave., Anchorage, AK 99501

Chugach National Forest (Portage, Columbia and Child's Glaciers)
P.O. Box 129, Girdwood, AK 99587

Denali National Park and Preserve (Muldrow Glacier)
P.O. Box 9, Denali Park, AK 99755

Glacier Bay National Park and Preserve (Muir Glacier)
Bartlett Cove, Gustavus, AK 99826-0140

Kenai Fjords National Park (Exit Glacier, Holgate Glacier)
P.O. Box 1727, Seward, AK 99664

Tongass National Forest (Mendenhall Glacier) Visitor Center
8465 Old Dairy Road, Juneau, AK 99801

Wrangell, St. Elias National Park (Malaspina and Hubbard Glaciers)
P.O. Box 29, Glennallen, AK 99588

The Alaska Natural History Association is an educational, non-profit
organization dedicated to supporting Alaska's public lands.